D1200298

DISCARD

DP 40

Bulldozers

by Charles Lennie

ABDO
CONSTRUCTION MACHINES
Kids

Visit us at www.abdopublishing.com

Published by Abdo Kids, a division of ABDO, P.O. Box 398166, Minneapolis, Minnesota 55439.

Copyright © 2015 by Abdo Consulting Group, Inc. International copyrights reserved in all countries. No part of this book may be reproduced in any form without written permission from the publisher.

Printed in the United States of America, North Mankato, Minnesota.

032014

092014

Photo Credits: iStock, Shutterstock, Thinkstock

Production Contributors: Teddy Borth, Jennie Forsberg, Grace Hansen

Design Contributors: Dorothy Toth, Renée LaViolette, Laura Rask

Library of Congress Control Number: 2013952430

Cataloging-in-Publication Data

Lennie, Charles.

 Bulldozers / Charles Lennie.

  p. cm. -- (Construction machines)

ISBN 978-1-62970-015-1 (lib. bdg.)

Includes bibliographical references and index.

1. Bulldozers--Juvenile literature. 2. Earthmoving machinery--Juvenile literature. 3. Excavating machinery--Juvenile literature. 4. Construction equipment--Juvenile literature. 5. Machinery--Juvenile literature. 6. Industrial equipment--Juvenile literature. I. Title.

624.152--dc23

2013952430

Table of Contents

Bulldozers

Bulldozers are important machines at construction sites.

Bulldozers move **materials**

like dirt and rocks.

Bulldozers help make the

ground **even**.

9

Bulldozers can even knock

things down!

Bulldozer Parts

The driver sits in the cab. There are special controls in the cab.

13

All bulldozers have a **blade**.

The blade is like a shovel.

15

Some bulldozers have rippers.

The ripper looks like a claw.

It breaks up hard ground.

17

Moving

Some bulldozers have special tires. But most have **tracks**.

19

Some **terrain** is hard to drive on. **Tracks** help bulldozers move easily.

21

More Facts

- The bulldozer began as a wooden **blade** pushed by humans or animals. It was used to flatten ground, especially for farming.

- Bulldozers are not very fast. Most people can walk faster than a bulldozer.

- Bulldozer operators need to know a lot about soil. They should also know how to deal with special situations, like moving large rocks and boulders.

Glossary

blade – attached to the body of a machine. It acts like a shovel.

cab – where the driver sits to control the machine.

even – flat, smooth.

material – anything used for construction, or making something else.

terrain – a piece of land having certain features.

tracks – continuous metal band around the wheels of a heavy vehicle.

23

Index

abdokids.com

Use this code to log on to abdokids.com and access crafts, games, videos and more!

Abdo Kids Code:
CBK0151